MUKHTASSAR AL-AKHDARI

THE FIQH OF THE ACTS OF WORSHIP ACCORDING TO THE MALIKI SCHOOL OF ISLAMIC LAW

BY IMAM ABDUR-RAHMAN AL-AKHDARI
1514 CE-1546 CE

TRANSLATED BY SIDI BAYE

© FAYDA BOOKS, PUBLISHING & DISTRIBUTION

ISBN 978-0-9913813-2-6

All rights reserved, no part of this publication may be produced, stored in a retrieval system or transmitted in any form or by any means, electronic, mechanical, photocopy, recording or otherwise, without the prior consent of the copyright holder.

First published 2014
Fayda books publishing & distribution
Atlanta, Georgia usa

Cover design by Muhammadan press

Printed in America

Table of Contents

ON THE JURISPRUDENCE OF ACTS OF WORSHIP ACCORDING TO THE SCHOOL i
OF IMAM MALIK BIN ANAS (May Allah be pleased with them both) i
FOREWARD v
INTRODUCTION vii

CHAPTER 1 1
  PRIMARY OBLIGATIONS 1
    THE FIRST OBLIGATION 1
    THINGS PROHIBITED 1

CHAPTER 2 5
  RITUAL PURIFICATION 5
    PURIFICATION IS OF TWO TYPES 5
    REMOVING IMPURITIES 5
    ACTS OF WUDHU (MINOR PURIFICATION) 6
      THE OBLIGATORY (FARD) ACTS OF WUDHU ARE SEVEN 6
      THE SUNNAH ACTS 6
      ITS VIRTUOUS ACTS 7
    THINGS THAT NULLIFY WUDHU 7
      THE IMPURITIES 7
      THE CAUSES 7
    THINGS PROHIBITED BY LACK OF WUDHU 8
    GHUSL (MAJOR PURIFICATION) 8
      JANABA IS CAUSED BY TWO THINGS 9
    ACTS OF GHUSL 9
      THE OBLIGATORY ACTS OF GHUSL 9
      THE SUNNAH ACTS 9
      THE VIRTUOUS ACTS 9
      THINGS PROHIBITED BY JUNUB PERSON 10
    TAYAMMUM (DRY ABLUTION) 10
      THE OBLIGATORY ACTS OF TAYAMMUM 11

- *THE SUNNAH ACTS* 11
- *THE VIRTUOUS ACTS* 11
- *THINGS THAT INVALIDATE TAYAMMUM* 12
- MENSTRUATION 12
- LOCHIA (POSTPARTUM BLEEDING) 13

CHAPTER 3 15
- SALAT (RITUAL PRAYER) 15
- TIMES OF SALAT 15
- TIMES NAAFILAH SALAT IS FORBIDDEN 16
- PRECONDITIONS OF SALAT 16
- ACTS OF SALAT 17
  - *THE OBLIGATORY ACTS OF SALAT* 17
  - *THE SUNNAH ACTS OF SALAAT* 18
  - *THE VIRTUOUS ACTS OF SALAAT* 19
  - *THINGS DISLIKED IN SALAT* 21
- SALAAT IS A LIGHT 21
- MANNERS OF PERFORMING SALAT 22
- MAKING UP FOR MISSED SALAT 23
- ON THE PROSTRATION OF FORGETFULNESS 24
- FORGETFULNESS IN NAAFILAH 32
- FORGETFULNESS ON THE PART OF THE IMAM 33

Foreword

We commence with a Statement made by Ibn Taymiyya (rahmatullahi alaihi) about the scholars of Madina and the Maliki Madhhab. Ironically, he was not a follower of the Maliki Madhhab, which means, this is a more objective view and uninfluenced by taqlid. He writes…

"The school which they established in the era of the Sahaba (radhi'Allahu anhu aj'ma'in), their followers and their follower's followers, is the soundest of all such schools, in the East and West, in its roots as well as its branches. Whoever gives careful thought to the fundamentals of Islam and the principles of Islamic Law will find that the fundamentals adhered to by Imam Malik (rahmatullahi alaihi) and the inhabitants of Madina were the soundest of all principles and rules. This is a vast topic, and if we were to do a thorough investigation of the merit of Madina's scholars and the soundness of their principles, we would have a great more to say. This said, there can be no doubt on anyone's part that of all people, no one has shown greater concern for the Madina school than Imam Malik (rahmatullahi alaihi) whether by transmitting the narratives through which it has been passed down by or by explaining its views. Indeed, neither in his own era nor since his era has anyone done more than Imam Malik (rahmatullahi alaihi) in this respect."

The Maliki Madhhab is a school with which the Imam, Malik ibn Anas (rahmatullahi alaihi), was associated and was only one of its numerous links. Even so, he was, both in his own era and thereafter, the one who possessed the most thorough understanding of this school and who undertook the most comprehensive collection of its supporting narratives.

Ibrahim Ahmed Dimson
Publisher, Fayda Books

INTRODUCTION

In the Name of Allah, the Compassionate the Merciful

All praise belongs to Allah, who commanded his servants who have believed to "Perform Salah…." Q14:31

May the prayer and peace of Allah be upon the light of the Divine Essence, our Master Muhammad who said, as recorded in Tabaranni "The first matter the slave will be brought to account for on the day of judgment is the prayer (Salah). If it is sound, the rest of his deeds will be sound, and if it is bad, then the rest of his deeds will be bad"

For this introduction, I have chosen to quote Mawlana, Shaykh al-Islam Alhajj Ibrahim Niass, may Allah be pleased with him, from his book Tawsi'at al-Ilm wal'Irfan;

"…The best act of worship is Salât, which is the second pillar of the deen which the chosen Prophet, peace be upon him, has built. If there was any act of worship better than Salât then the Angels would have done it, but the Angels in heaven, all of them, pray with perpetual bowing, prostration and standing. The most important pre-requisite of Salât is purification; either Ghusl (bath) or Wudhu (ablution). As for ritual purification, an indication of its importance is gained by studying the life of Imam Shafi, one of the four Imams of Sunni jurisprudence. Whenever Imam Shafi is about to make Wudhu you will see a look of terror on his face when he was asked about it, he said 'The look you see is due to the fact that I'm about to stand for intimate discourse with Allah and whenever a King invites a man into his court in order to honor him, the man will take necessary precaution to prepare for such an audience." This is why we make Wudhu before Salât and why we make sure our clothes are clean, because we know we are about to stand in the presence of Allah. Then we say Allahuakbar and raise our hands…what is the meaning of this? We intend by this to cast the world and what it contains behind us, saying that Allah is greater than you and everything you contain. If a person understands the meaning of Allahuakbar, they will be completely free in this dunya (world) because everything you are afraid of…Allah is greater than it. Likewise, everything you love and are seeking…Allah is greater than it…"

Shaykh al-Islam Alhajj Ibrahim Niass
From his book, "Tawsi'at al-'Ilm wal' Irfan'

CHAPTER 1: PRIMARY OBLIGATIONS

THE FIRST OBLIGATION

The first obligation upon an adult is the correction of his Faith, then acquiring knowledge of that which is incumbent for the proper performance of his personal duties, such as the rules governing *Salât* (ritual Prayer), *Taharah* (ritual purification) and *Sawm* (fasting).

It is also obligatory on him to keep strictly within the limits set by Allah by executing His commands and avoiding His prohibitions. He should also complete his repentance to Allah, the Exalted, before Allah's wrath reaches him.

The conditions of repentance however, are deep remorse for past wrongdoings and the resolve never to return to sin for the rest of one's life with an immediate abstinence from disobedience if one is still involved in such actions. It is not right for him to delay the process of repentance and to say, "I will repent whenever Allah guides me". Such statements are only signs of misery, self-debasement and lack of spiritual insight.

It is also obligatory on the adult to safeguard his tongue from indecent and abusive speech, swearing by divorce[1], abusing, humiliating, insulting or frightening a fellow Muslim without any legitimate (*Shar'i*) reason.

It is obligatory on him to avert his eyes from looking at things forbidden just as it is not right for him to look at a Muslim with

---

1 This refers to a certain bad habit some people have of saying for example: "If I do not do such and such a thing I would divorce my wife."

مختصر الأخضري

the intent to harm him unless this person is a deviant, in which case they should be shunned.

It is also obligatory on him to safeguard his limbs against all evil acts to the best of his ability. He should also love for the sake of Allah alone, abhor for His sake and be pleased or annoyed for His sake. He should likewise enjoin the good and decent while forbidding the bad and indecent.

THINGS PROHIBITED

It is forbidden for him to lie, backbite, maliciously gossip, and be proud and arrogant. It is likewise forbidden for him to show off for the sake of appearance and reputation, be envious and hateful or brag about his favors on others. Also forbidden are scornfulness and mockery as well as caricaturing and ridiculing others.

Adultery and fornication are also forbidden, so is looking lustfully at a woman not one's wife or to take pleasure in her speech. It is also forbidden to consume peoples' wealth without their consent or to make ones living through corrupt legal practices or the abuse of religion.

Likewise forbidden is to delay the *Salât and* thereby missing the prescribed time.

It is not permissible for him to keep the company of a wrongdoer (*faasiq*) or to sit with him without necessity nor should he seek the pleasure of the creation, at the expense of incurring the displeasure of the Creator.

مختصر الأخضري

> **Allah, the Exalted,** has said:
> *"...Allah and His Messenger are most worthy of being pleased if indeed they are Believers".*
> *(Qur'an: Surah 9: Verse 62)*
>
> **The Messenger,** (May Allah grant him peace), also said:
> *"No created being has the right to be obeyed at the expense of disobedience to the Creator"*
>
> *(Sahih Al-Bukhari)*

It is not permissible for him to undertake any deed except after he knows the ruling of Allah concerning that matter. He should, as a matter of duty, ask the learned and follow the examples of those who follow the traditions (Sunnah) of Prophet Muhammad (May Allah exalt his mention and grant him peace). Such are people who lead others unto the way of obedience to Allah and warn against following satan (shaitan). He should not be content to choose for himself what the morally corrupt have chosen, and whose lives have been lost in acts of disobedience to Allah, the Exalted. How great their despair and how long their wailings on the Day of Judgment!

We pray to Allah to enable us to follow the Sunnah (traditions) of our Prophet, Intercessor, and Master Muhammad (May Allah exalt his mention and grant him peace).

CHAPTER 2: RITUAL PURIFICATION

PURIFICATION IS OF TWO TYPES

Minor and Major purification, neither of which can be properly done except by means of water which must be pure and purifying. That means all its basic elements of color, taste and smell have not been altered by a foreign agent such as oil, fat, yeast of all types or foam, soap, dirt and the like.

There is however, no harm with sand, mud, salt, earth, fur or the like.

REMOVING IMPURITIES

If an impurity touches a place, the affected section(s) must be washed with water. If it becomes difficult to determine the spot(s) then wash the entire garment. If however, one simply suspects being touched by impurity then it is enough to sprinkle water on the clothing. If one doubts the purity of a thing that touches him, no sprinkling is necessary.

He who remembers an impurity while in *Salât*, must immediately interrupt his *Salât* unless he fears missing the prescribed time. He who forgetfully does *Salât* with an impurity and remembers only after *Salaam*, must repeat the *Salât* as long as it is still within time.

مختصر الأخضري

ACTS OF WUDHU[2] (MINOR PURIFICATION)

THE OBLIGATORY (FARD) ACTS OF WUDHU ARE SEVEN:

the intention, washing the face, washing the hands up to the elbows, wiping over the head (with wet hands), washing the feet up to the ankles, scrubbing (while washing) and doing it fast.

THE SUNNAH ACTS ARE:

washing the hands up to the wrists at the beginning, rinsing the mouth, inhaling water into the nostrils and exhaling, returning the wiping of the head, wiping over the ears and renewing water to do so and doing the Obligatory acts in the prescribed order.

Whoever forgets to wash an Obligatory part of his limbs and remembers before long should then wash it and rewash all the parts that follow it. If however he remembers only after a long time, he should then wash it alone and repeat all *Salats* he made before. If however, the part forgotten is *Sunnah*, it should be washed alone with no repetition of *Salât*.

He who leaves a spot unwashed should wash only that area upon remembrance with intention (of *Wudhu*). Any *Salât* done before that should be repeated. He who remembers having left out the rinsing of his mouth or the inhaling of water after already starting with the face should not go back to the forgotten parts until he finishes his ablution.

---

2 This is the Arabic for Ablution.

مختصر الأخضري

ITS VIRTUOUS ACTS ARE:

Reciting the "Basmalah"[3], tooth brushing[4], washing the face and hands more than once, beginning from the forehead when wiping over the head, doing the Sunnah acts in the right order (see above), economizing the use of water on the limbs, starting with the right before the left. It is obligatory to wet in between the fingers while it is recommended to do the same with the toes. It is also obligatory to wet ones beard during ablution when it is lightly grown, not when it is thick. In ritual bath (Ghusl) however, even thick beard must be thoroughly wet.

THINGS THAT NULLIFY WUDHU

Ablution (*Wudhu*) is nullified by either ritual impurities or causes thereof.

The impurities are:

Urine, feces, breaking wind, emitting prostatic fluid and genital discharges.

The causes are:

Deep sleep, unconsciousness, intoxication, insanity, kissing, touching the opposite sex if pleasure is either intended or derived, touching the penis with the inside of the palm or the fingers.

---

3 Bismillaahir Rahmaanir Rahim.

4 It is best done with the traditional chewing stick before each Wudhu.

مختصر الأخضري

Whoever has doubts about impurity must renew his *Wudhu* unless it is a whispering coming from Shaitan, in which case he need not do anything. The whole penis must be washed in case of the secretion of prostatic fluid but not the testicles. Prostatic fluid is the liquid secreted when aroused through fantasizing, lustful looks or the like.

THINGS PROHIBITED BY LACK OF WUDHU

It is not permissible for one without *Wudhu* to perform *Salât*, *Tawaaf*,[5] touch a copy of the Mighty Qur'an or even its cover whether with his hands or even with a stick or the like, except a part of it for one learning form it. A board on which the Qur'an is written should likewise not be touched without *Wudhu* except by one learning from it or a teacher tutoring him.

The same rules apply to a child touching the Qur'an given to him by an adult, except that the sin incurred shall be on the adult who gave him access to it.

Whoever performs *Salât* without *Wudhu*, intentionally, is a disbeliever. We seek refuge in Allah.

GHUSL (MAJOR PURIFICATION)

Ghusl (ritual bath) is obligatory on account of three things:
Janaaba,[6] menstruation and postnatal bleeding.

---

5 Circumambulation of the Kaaba.

6 Major impurity.

مختصر الأخضري

JANABA IS CAUSED BY TWO THINGS:

1. The release of semen with normal pleasure while asleep or awake by intercourse or any other means.
2. The other arises immediately when the glans of the male organ penetrates the female genitalia.

Whoever sees himself having intercourse in a dream but does not release any semen has nothing to worry about. Whoever finds dry sperm on his garment and cannot remember when it got there should perform *Ghusl* and repeat all *Salât* he has done since the last time he slept.

ACTS OF GHUSL

THE OBLIGATORY ACTS OF GHUSL ARE:

The intention when beginning, doing it fast, scrubbing and washing the whole body.

THE SUNNAH ACTS ARE:

Washing the hands up to the wrists as in Wudhu, rinsing the mouth, inhaling water into the nostrils and exhaling, washing the inner parts of the ear, as to the lower lobes of the ears it is obligatory to wash them back and front.

THE VIRTUOUS ACTS ARE:

Beginning with washing the impurity[7], then the private part, making your intention at this point, then washing the parts of

---

7 In practice, that is the area between the navel (belly-button) and the knees.

مختصر الأخضري

Wudhu once each, then the upper parts of the body and washing the head three times; doing the right sections of the body before the left, using as little water as possible.

Whoever forgets a spot or limb during his *Ghusl* must hasten to do so as soon as he remembers, even if that takes a month. He should then repeat all the *Salats* done before. If he delays the washing after such remembrance then the *Ghusl* itself becomes void. If however, the part(s) forgotten are among those washed in *Wudhu*, then the *Wudhu* washing(s) would suffice.

THINGS PROHIBITED BY JANABA

One in a state of janaba is not permitted to enter the Masjid or recite the Qur'an except an Aayat or the like for seeking protection or the like.

It is likewise not permissible for one who is inhibited from using cold water to have intercourse with his spouse unless he makes ample arrangements (for hot water). If he has wet dreams however, there is no blame on him (for not washing).

TAYAMMUM (DRY ABLUTION)

Tayammum is done by a traveler not on a mission of disobedience to Allah, and the sick person for *Fard* (obligatory) as well as *Naafilah* (voluntary) *Salats*. The healthy resident may also do *Tayammum* for a *Fard Salât* if he fears missing the prescribed time. The healthy resident cannot however, do *Tayammum* for

مختصر الأخضري

a *Naafilah*, *Jumu'ah*[8] or *Janaza*[9] *Salats* unless if none but him can perform the *Janaaza*.

THE OBLIGATORY ACTS OF TAYAMMUM ARE:

The intention, pure earth, wiping over the face, and the hands up to the wrists, striking the soil the first time, doing it fast, doing it within the prescribed time of Salât and immediately before the actual Salât.

By pure earth is meant: sand, sun-dried bricks, stone, snow, mud, and the like.

Tayammum is not permissible on whitewashed (or painted) walls, mats, wood, grass and the like. An allowance is made for a sick person to do it on a stone or sun-dried brick wall if there is no one to fetch him something else.

THE SUNNAH ACTS ARE:

Striking the earth once again with the hands, wiping over the forearm: between the wrists and elbows and following the order thus prescribed.

THE VIRTUOUS ACTS ARE:

Reciting the "Basmalah", doing the right before the left, doing the back of the forearm before the inner part and its front before its end.

---

8 This is the Friday Congregational Salât.
9 This is the Funeral Salât.

مختصر الأخضري

THINGS THAT INVALIDATE TAYAMMUM

The same things that invalidate *Wudhu* also invalidate *Tayammum*. You cannot perform two *Fard* (obligatory) *Salats* with one *Tayammum*. However, if one does *Tayammum* for a *Fard Salât* it becomes permissible for him thereafter to perform any amount of *Naafilah Salats* with it. He could also touch The Quran, do *Tawaaf* and recite The Quran if he had intended any of these and did it immediately after the *Salât* and before the end of the prescribed time. All of the things mentioned above except *Fard Salât* could also be done with the *Tayammum* for a *Naafilah Salât*. Whoever prays *Isha* with *Tayammum* can arise immediately thereafter and perform the *Shaf'* and *Witr Salât* without delay. Whoever has the need to perform *Tayammum* while in a state of *Janaaba* must include this in his intention.

MENSTRUATION

Women are grouped into three categories as far as menstruation is concerned:

1. First time beginners.

2. Regularly menstruating women.

3. Pregnant women.

The maximum length of menstruation for a first time beginner is 15 days. For the regularly menstruating woman it is her normal period. If however, the blood continues to come she adds three days at a time for as long as it does not exceed 15 days. For the pregnant woman the maximum is fifteen days when she is over three months pregnant. After six months

مختصر الأخضري

of pregnancy it becomes twenty days. If the bleeding stops at intervals she puts the days together until she completes her normal period.[10]

It is not permissible for a menstruating woman to perform *Salât*, fast, do *Tawaaf*, touch the Qur'an or enter the Masjid. She must however, make up for the fasting but not the *Salât*. Her recitation of the Qur'an is permissible. Her husband however, is not allowed to touch her private parts or anything between her navel and her knees until she has had *Ghusl*.

LOCHIA (POSTPARTUM BLEEDING)

Postpartum bleeding is the same as menstruation as far as the things it prohibits are concerned. Its maximum duration is sixty days. If however, the bleeding happens to stop even on the day of delivery she should perform *Ghusl* and observe her *Salats*. In case the bleeding starts again and fifteen days or more have passed then the second is menstrual blood. If it is less than fifteen days then it must be counted with the first until the lochia is completed.

---

10 The rules regarding irregular periods vary greatly from one jurist to another. However, the minimum period of purity between periods is fifteen days.

CHAPTER 3
SALAT (RITUAL PRAYER)

TIMES OF SALAT[11]

The Prime Time for *Zuhr* (*The Afternoon Salât*) is from the time the sun begins to decline from its meridian to the time when the shadow of everything reaches its full length.

The Prime Time for *Asr* (*The Late Afternoon Salât*) is from the time the shadow reaches its full length to the time the sun turns yellow.

The Extended Time for both *Salats* lasts up to sunset.

The Prime Time for *Maghrib* (*The early Evening Salât*) is calculated by the time it actually takes to perform it after its preconditions have been fulfilled.

The Prime Time for *Isha* (*The Night Salât*) is from the disappearance of the twilight glow up to the end of the first third of the night.

The Extended Time for both *Salats* lasts until the rise of dawn.

The Prime Time for *Subh* (*The Morning*) or *Fajr* (*Dawn*) *Salât* is from dawn until the first brightening. Its Extended Time lasts until sunrise.

---

11 Each individual Salât has its time divided into two: Ikhtiyaari (Prime or Preferred) and Dharoori (Extended or Allocated). These two times together constitute what the Qur'anic Aayat 103 in Surah An-Nisaa denotes: "…establish Regular Salât: For such Salats are enjoined on believers at stated times.

مختصر الأخضري

Making up for missed *Salât* in all cases happens when these times have elapsed. Whoever delays *Salât* until its time passes *(both Prime & Extended)*, would incur a grave sin except for one who did so forgetfully or was asleep.[12]

TIMES NAAFILAH SALAT IS FORBIDDEN

No *Naafilah Salât* is permitted after the *Subh Salât* until after the sun has risen high. It is also not done after the *Asr Salât* till the time of *Maghrib* and after the rise of dawn except *Wird Salât*[13] (regular litanies) for one who oversleeps.

Naafilah Salât is also not done when the Imam of the *Jumu'ah Salât* sits on the *Mimbar*[14] (pulpit) and after the *Jumu'ah Salât* itself until one leaves the *Masjid*.

PRECONDITIONS OF SALAT

The preconditions of *Salât* are: purification of the body, clothing and place (of worship) from both minor and major impurities[15]. Also, preconditions are to cover the private parts, fac-

---

12 Delaying Salât is also permissible for one who is sick or on a journey: the latter is governed by special rules.

13 This is for one who has a well established routine of performing a set of Rak'at (units of Salât) every night. The permission however, is valid only if there is enough time for the Subh Salât before sunrise and one can still make the Jamaa'at at the Masjid.

14 No naafilah, talking or gesturing is permitted at this time.

15 Minor impurities are those that necessitate only Wudhu while major impurities are those that necessitate Ghusl.

مختصر الأخضري

ing the *Qibla (direction of the Kaaba)*, refraining from talking and unnecessary motion.

The private parts of a man are what lie between the navel and the knees. For the woman all her body is considered private except her face and hands.

It is abhorrent to do *Salât* in underwear except if something is worn over them. Whoever has an impurity on his clothing and cannot find another nor does he find water to wash it or another to wear while the impure one is washed and fears missing the time; he should do *Salât* with the impurity. Delaying *Salât* because of an impurity is not permitted and whoever does so would disobey his Lord. Whoever does not find enough clothing to cover their private parts should do *Salât* naked.

Whoever mistakes the *Qibla* should repeat his *Salât* only if it is still within time. Every such repetition of *Salât* within time is considered a virtuous act. Repetition of *Salât* within time does not however, include missed or *Naafilah Salât.*

ACTS OF SALAT

THE OBLIGATORY ACTS OF SALAT ARE:

The intention for the specific Salât, the Takbir-at-ul-Ihraam[16] and standing while doing so, reciting Surah-al-Fâtiha and standing while doing so, the Ruku' (bowing) and standing up straight

---

16 This is the first utterance of 'Allahu Akbar' at the commencement of Salât.

مختصر الأخضري

thereafter, the Sujud (prostration) on the forehead and arising therefrom; doing every act with due serenity and tranquility as well as doing these obligatory acts in the right sequence. The Salaam and staying in the sitting position while uttering it are also both obligatory.

The condition for the validity of the intention however, is done simultaneously with the *Takbir-at-ul-Ihraam.**

THE SUNNAH ACTS OF SALAAT ARE:

The Iqaama[17], the Surah recited after Al- Fâtiha and standing while doing so, reciting silently in that which should be silent and audibly in that which should be audible. It is also a Sunnah act to say Sami'al-Laahu liman Hamida[18].

All *Takbirs*[19] except the first one are *Sunnah*, so are the two *Tashahhuds*[20] and sitting down to do so as well as beginning with the recitation of *Fâtiha* before the *Surah*. The second and third pronouncements of *Salaam*[21] by one doing *Salât* behind an Imam are *Sunnah* as well as saying the obligatory *Salaam* aloud.

---

17 This is the second call to Salât followed immediately by the Takbir-at-ul-Ihraam. It is a Sunnah act for men and a meritorious act for women.

18 'Allah hears those who thank Him': said when arising from the Ruku' posture.

19 Utterances of 'Allahu Akbar'(Allah is Greatest).

20 *"Attahiyyaatu liLaahi, Azzaakiyaatu liLaahi, Attayyibaatu was-Salawaatu liLaahi. Assalaamu Alaika Ayyuhan-Nabiyyu wa Rahmatul Laahi wa Barakaatuhu. Assalaamu Alainaa wa Alaa Ibaadil-Laahis- Saalihina. Ash-hadu an laa Ilaaha illal-Laahu Wahdahu laa Sharika lahu wa Ash-hadu anna Muhammadan Abduhu wa Rasooluhu."* This is recited after every two Rak'at, (always before Salaam).

21 This is the case in which the obligatory Salaam is pronounced towards the

مختصر الأخضري

Sunnah acts also include invoking blessings on the Messenger of Allah[22] (May Allah exalt his mention and grant him peace) and making *Sujud* on the nose, the palms of the hands, the knees and the tips of the toes. The *Sutra*[23] (barrier) for one not doing *Salât* behind an Imam is also *Sunnah*. The *Sutra* should at least be of the thickness of a spear and the length of a forearm, pure, stationary and not distracting.

THE VIRTUOUS ACTS OF SALAAT ARE:

Raising the hands to the level of the ears in Takbir-at-ul-Ihraam, saying Rabbanaa wa Lakal Hamd[24] by one following an Imam or doing Salât alone, saying Aameen[25] after the recitation of Al-Fâtiha if one is alone or behind an Imam. The Imam himself says it only in Salât with silent recitation.[26]

Qibla and the other two which are Sunnah are said while turning towards the right then left. However, the most common form is to pronounce two Salaams beginning by saying the first one towards the Qibla and finishing it while turning right and doing the same again while turning left.

22 "*Allaahumma Salli alaa Sayyidinaa Muhammadin wa alaa Aali Sayyidinaa Muhammadin kamaa Sallaita alaa Sayyidinaa Ibraahima wa alaa Sayyidinaa Ibraahima wa Baarik alaa Sayyidinaa Muhammadin wa alaa Sayyidinaa Muhammadin kamaa Baarakta alaa Sayyidinaa Ibraahima wa alaa Aali Sayyidinaa Ibraahima fil Aalamina Innaka Hamidun Majiid.*" This is recited after the second Tashhahud before Salaam.

23 This is an object a person doing Salât alone places before him/her to allow others pass in front of him/her without hindrance.

24 'Our Lord; and praise be to You.' This is said when arising from Ruku' in response to "*Sami'al-Laahu liman Hamidahu.*"

25 This means: 'Oh Lord! Answer our prayers'.

26 Opinions differ on this point. According to other jurists the Imam says it as well even in audible recitation.

مختصر الأخضري

Virtuous acts also include glorification of Allah in *Ruku'*[27] and supplication in *Sujud*[28] as well as lengthening the recitation in *Subh* and *Zuhr* (the latter being a bit shorter), shortening it in *Asr* and *Maghrib* and making it medium in *Isha*. The *Surah* in the first *Rak'at* should be before the one in the second (*i.e. according to their order in the Qur'an*) it, the first, should also be longer than the second. The known form[29] for *Ruku'*, *Sujud* and sitting as well as reciting the *Du'aa-ul-Qunut*[30] silently are all virtuous acts. The *Qunut* is recited in *Subh* after the *Surah* and before *Ruku'* although it is also permissible after *Ruku'*. Additional

supplications after the second *Tashahhud*, making it longer than the first and turning towards the right while pronouncing the *Salaam* as well as moving (or pointing straight with) the index finger during *Tashahhud* are all virtuous acts.

---

27 Saying:"**Subhaana Rabbi-al-Adheem wa Bi Hamdihi**" (three times) meaning: 'Glory be to my Lord, the Greatest and His is all Praise.'

28 Saying:"**Subhaana Rabbi-al-A'alaa wa Bi Hamdihi**" (three times) meaning: 'Glory be to my Lord, the Most High and His is all Praise ' plus any Du'aas that you know especially from the Prophet (s.a.w).

29 That is the established postures: placements of the limbs such as the hands on the knees and bending the back straight without lifting the head or bending it too far downwards in Ruku'.

30 *"Allaahumma inna nasta'eenuka wa nastaghfiruka wa nu'uminu bika wa natawakkalu Alaika wa Nakhna'u Laka wa nakhla'u wa natruku man yakfuruka. Allaahumma Iyyaaka na'abud wa Laka nusallii wa nasjud wa Ilaika nas'aa wa nahfid. Narrjoo Rahmataka wa nakhaafu Azhaabaka-l-Jidda. Inna Azhaabaka bil kaafireena mulhiq."*

مختصر الأخضري

THINGS DISLIKED IN SALAT

It is disliked to look about in *Salât*, close ones eyes or begin recitation with the *Basmalah* and *Isti'aazha* (*i.e. saying: A'oozhu – bil – Laahi minas Shaytanir Rajeem*) in *Fard Salât*[31]. Both are however, allowed in *Nafilah*. It is also disliked to stand on one leg in *Salât* except

if one has been standing for a very long time. Also disliked is to keep the feet tight together or to put a coin or any other thing in ones mouth. Likewise anything that can cause distraction in ones pocket, sleeves or on the back. Similarly, engaging ones mind with thought about worldly affairs and everything that may divert ones attention from humbleness before Allah in *Salât*.

SALAAT IS A LIGHT

Salât has immense Divine lights which illuminate the hearts of those who perform it and none attain to it except those who are aware and humble themselves before Allah. Therefore if you come to perform *Salât*, empty your heart of all things worldly and engage yourself with awareness of your Lord for Whose Countenance you pray. Keep in mind that *Salât* is in fact a matter of awe and humility before Allah, the Exalted in standing still, bowing, prostrating, exhibiting unequalled

---

31 This is also another matter of contention even among jurists within the Maliki School itself, renowned Maliki Mujtahid, Shaykh Ibrahim Niass has issued fatawa supporting the loud recitation and continual flow of the Basmalla with …alhamdulilah rabil alamin, for further elaboration please see Raf'al Malaam…

مختصر الأخضري

respect and esteem for Him by means of *Takbir* (*see note 18*), *Tasbih* (*glorification*) and *Zhikr* (*constant remembrance and adoration*). Guard therefore, your *Salât*. It is the greatest form of worship. Do not allow *Shaitan* to play with your heart and distract you from your *Salât* thereby obliterating your heart and depriving you from enjoying the Divine Lights of *Salât*. Be constantly mindful; humbling yourself in *Salât* for that way it protects from all shameful and blameworthy deeds. Seek help through Allah for He is the best to seek help from.

MANNERS OF PERFORMING SALAT

There are seven different manners of performing *Fard Salât*. Four of these are done by way of obligation and the other three by way of recommendation.

Those done by way of obligation are:

Standing without support, then standing with support, then sitting without support, then sitting with support.

Performing *Salât* in one of these manners and in the given order is a matter of obligation. If one is able to do it in the one manner but chooses instead to do it in a subordinate manner then their *Salât* is void.

The three that are by way of recommendation are:

That the disabled should perform Salât in one of these three manners: lying on his right side or on his left side or on his back. He is free to choose whichever of them is most convenient for him.

مختصر الأخضري

The support which invalidates the *Salât* of the one who is able to dispense with it is such that he would fall if it fell. If he will not fall by the falling of the support then it becomes reprehensible.

As to the *Naafilah Salât* it is permissible for the one able to stand to perform it sitting but he will only get half the reward. It is likewise permissible to enter the *Salât* in a sitting position and stand up afterwards or to enter it standing and to sit down afterwards unless one had the specific intention of performing it standing then he should refrain from sitting down afterwards.

MAKING UP FOR MISSED SALAT

All missed (*Fard*) *Salât* must be made up. It is not permissible to be negligent in this matter. Whoever makes *Salât* for five consecutive days is not negligent. *Salât* must be repaid in the same manner it was missed: if it was missed while resident it should be repaid as such and if it was on a journey[32] it should be repaid as such and it makes no difference whether at the time of repayment one is resident or on a journey. Maintaining the right order between two concurrent *Salats*[33] as well as between a few missed ones and a current one is obligatory if one so remembers. By a few, it is meant four *Salats* or less.

---

32 This refers to the shortening of Salât while travelling. When on a journey of at least 70km in distance one is normally allowed to shorten four Rak'at Salats to two, etc.

33 This is as in the case of Zuhr and Asr which share the same Extended Time. See times of Salât above.

مختصر الأخضري

Whoever has missed four *Salats* or less should make up for them before the current one even if that would make him miss the time of the current one also. Making up for *Salât* is permissible at all times. He who has (*Fard*) *Salât(s)* to make up for does not do *Naafilah* nor does he do *Dhuhaa*, (the forenoon *Salât*) or *Ramadhan* night *Salats* (*Tarawih*). No other *Salats* would be permissible for him except *shaf* and *Al-Witr*[34], the *Sunnah* of *Fajr*, the two *Eid Salats*, the eclipse *Salât* and the special *Salât* for rain during severe droughts.

It is permissible for those who are making up for missed *Salât(s)* to observe them together if their missed *Salats* are the same and whoever forgets the number of *Salats* they have missed should make up for a number that would be enough to remove any doubts.

ON THE PROSTRATION OF FORGETFULNESS

The (*Sujud*)[35] of forgetfulness in *Salât* is a *Sunnah* act. For acts of *Salât* omitted two *Sujud* (*Sajdatain*) are made before *Salaam* after the completion of the two *Tashahhuds*. Another *Tashahhud* is then recited and *Salaam* made again. For additions two *Sujuds* are made after *Salaam*. The *Tashahhud* should then be repeated and *Salaam* made.

---

34 These are the three Rak'at of emphatic Sunnah one offers after Isha or as a closing for all Salats of the day and night before Fajr.

35 "Sujud" is the act of prostration. "Sajda" is one Sujud and two Sujuds are "Sajdatain".

مختصر الأخضري

Whoever both adds and omits acts in *Salât* should perform *Sujud* before *Salaam*. Whoever forgets *Sujud* before *Salaam* till he utters the *Salaam* can still make it if it was recent. If however, it took a long time or he had already left the Masjid then the *Sujud* would become nullified and with it the entire *Salât*. That is if the act(s) involved constituted three *Sunnahs* or more. Otherwise, the *Salât* would still be valid. Whoever, on the other hand, forgets the *Sujud* before *Salaam* should make it immediately even if it had taken a whole year.

Whoever omits an obligatory (*Fard*) act however, cannot fix it with *Sujud*. For omissions relating to virtuous acts (*Fadhaa'il*) no *Sujud* is required.

Sujud before *Salaam* is not done except for the omission of two *Sunnah* acts or more. As to omitting a single *Sunnah* act, there is no *Sujud* for it except in the case of silent and audible recitations in *Salât*. Whoever recites silently in place of audible recitation should do *Sujud* before *Salaam* and whoever recites audibly in place of silent recitation should do *Sujud* after *Salaam*.

Whoever talks forgetfully in *Salât* should do *Sujud* after *Salaam*. Whoever pronounces the *Salaam* forgetfully after only two *Rak'at* should do *Sujud* after *Salaam*. Whoever adds a *Rak'at* or two *Rak'at* in *Salât* should do *Sujud* after *Salaam*. If however, one doubles the number of *Rak'at* then his *Salât* is nullified.

Whoever is unsure as to the completion of his *Salât* should do the acts he is unsure about. Doubts concerning omissions should be resolved accordingly. Whoever is thus unsure about doing a *Rak'at* or a *Sajda* (prostration) should do so immediately and then perform the *Sujud* after *Salaam*. If the doubt is

مختصر الأخضري

about the pronouncement of *Salaam* then it should be pronounced if the time was recent without any *Sujuds*. If however, a long time has passed then the *Salât* itself becomes invalid.

The habitually doubtful, should put aside his doubts and not redo any acts he is unsure of. He should however, always do the *Sujud* after *Salaam* regardless of whether his doubt is about an addition or an omission.

Whoever recites the *Du'aa–ul–Qunut*[36] aloud does not need to perform any *Sujuds* although it is abhorrent to do so deliberately. Similarly, there are no *Sujusd* on one who adds a *Surah* (*after Fâtiha*) in the last two *Rak'at* (*of a four Rak'at Salât*).

If one hears the name of *Muhammad*, (*May Allah exalt his mention and grant him peace*) mentioned while in *Salât* and says audibly, the blessing on him, he has nothing on him whether that was done forgetfully or intentionally, standing or sitting.

Whoever recites two *Surahs* or more in a single *Rak'at* or jumps from one *Surah* to another or goes to *Ruku'* before completing the *Surah* there is nothing on him in all of that. Whoever makes a gesture with his hands or head while in *Salât*, also has no fault on him.

Whoever repeats the *Fâtiha* forgetfully should perform the *Sujud* after *Salaam*. If however, this was done deliberately then the *Salât* most probably is invalid. If one remembers the *Surah* only after bending for *Ruku'*, he should not return to recite it. Whoever remembers silent or audible recitation before bending for *Ruku'* should repeat the whole recitation. If it con-

---

36 See note 29 above.

مختصر الأخضري

cerned only the *Surah*, he should repeat it without *Sujuds*. however, it involved the *Fâtiha* then he repeats it and performs the *Sujud* after *Salaam*. If however, he missed all that because he is already in *Ruku'* he should perform *Sujud* before *Salaam* for omitting audible recitation or after *Salaam* for silent recitation. This concerns both *Fâtiha* and the *Surah*.

Whoever laughs in *Salât* whether forgetfully or deliberately his *Salât* becomes invalid; and none laughs in his *Salât* except one who is negligent and playful. As to the Believer whenever he stands for *Salât*, he would turn with his heart away from all else except Allah, the Exalted. He leaves the world and all that it contains so that he is present with his heart and mind in the Majesty of Allah and His Greatness. His heart trembles and his soul is filled with terror in awe of Allah, the Exalted and Mighty. This is the *Salât* of the pious.

There is nothing wrong in smiling; while the crying in *Salât* of the humbly submissive (to Allah) is forgiven and one who pauses for a while to listen to a speaker has done no harm.

Whoever arises before sitting after two *Rak'at* and remembers before his hands and knees have left the ground he should return to the sitting position and no *Sujuds* would be necessary. If however, he has already left the ground he should proceed without returning to the sitting position and then does the *Sujud* before *Salaam*. However, if he still returns to sitting after leaving the ground either forgetfully or intentionally his *Salât* would be valid but he should do the *Sujud* after *Salaam*.

مختصر الأخضري

Whoever blows[37] in his *Salât* forgetfully should do the *Sujud* after *Salam*. If however, this is done deliberately his *Salât* becomes invalid. Whosoever sneezes in *Salât* needs not busy himself with saying *"Al Hamdu Lillah"* (praise be to Allah) nor does he respond to one who blesses him or bless one who sneezes. If however, he should choose to praise Allah there shall be no blame on him. Whoever yawns in *Salât* should cover his mouth and must not release any discharges except into his clothing while avoiding the articulation of any intelligible sounds.

Whoever has doubts about ritual impurity[38] or something impure[39], and reflects a little in his

Salât and then feels certain that he is clean, there shall be no fault on him.

Whoever looks about forgetfully in *Salât* there shall be non-fault on him. If however, this is done deliberately then it becomes a reprehensible act. If as much as turns away from the direction of the *Qibla* then he has broken his *Salât*. Whoever does *Salât* while wearing silk or gold or steals in *Salât* or looks at something forbidden he has disobeyed (his Lord) although his *Salât* is valid.

Whoever commits an error of recitation with a word not of the Qur'an he must do *Sujud* after *Salaam*. If however, the mistaken word is of the Qur'an then there is no *Sujud* on him

---

37 This is expelling breath loudly.

38 An impurity like urine, mucus or foul air from oneself.

39 An impure foreign agent touching his body or clothing.

مختصر الأخضري

unless he alters the phrase or spoils the meaning, then he does the *Sujud* after *Salaam*.

Whoever dozes off in *Salât* owes no *Sujuds*. If however, he sleeps heavily then he must repeat both the *Salât* and *Wudhu*.

The groaning of the sick is forgiven and clearing ones throat out of necessity is excused while doing so in order to convey a message is improper although it does not invalidate *Salât*. If one in *Salât* responds to a caller by saying "*Subhâna'llâh*" (glory be to Allah) it is disliked, yet his *Salât* remains valid.

Whoever stops in recitation and no one prompts him, should leave that *Aayat* and read the one after it. If he is unable to do so then he should proceed to *Ruku'* and not look at a copy of the Qur'an before him unless it be in the *Fâtiha* in which case it must be completed either by using a copy of the Qur'an or something else. If he omits an *Aayat* of the *Fâtiha*, he does the

Sujud before *Salaam*. If however, more than an *Aayat* is omitted, then the *Salât* becomes invalid.

Whoever prompts an Imam other than the one behind whom he is worshipping has invalidated his *Salât*. One does not in fact prompt his Imam unless he waits to be prompted or alters the meaning.

If ones mind wonders a little into worldly affairs his reward lessens but his *Salât* is not invalidated.

Whoever pushes away someone about to pass in front of him or makes *Sujud* on the side of his forehead or on a roll or two

مختصر الأخضري

rolls of his turban there is nothing on him. There is likewise, no harm for involuntary vomiting or belching in *Salât*.

The forgetfulness of the follower in *Salât* is borne by the Imam except it be a case of omitting a *Fard* (obligatory) act.

If one following an Imam in *Salât* forgets or dozes off or is pressed for time to make the *Ruku'* in other than the first *Rak'at* and he hopes to catch up with the Imam before the latter arises from the second *Sajda*, he should go to *Ruku'* and then join the Imam. If however, he has no such hope of catching up with the Imam, he skips the *Ruku'* and follows his Imam and then makes up an extra *Rak'at* to replace this one after the Imam's *Salaam*.

If on the other hand, he forgets the *Sujud* or is pressed for time or dozes off until the Imam stands up for the next *Rak'at*, he should go to *Sujud* even if he desires to catch up with the Imam before the latter goes to *Ruku'*. Otherwise, he skips it and follows the Imam and makes up for this later with an additional *Rak'at*. When he has made up with the additional *Rak'at*, no *Sujuds* would be required of him unless he has doubts concerning the *Ruku'* or *Sujud*.

Whoever is approached by a scorpion or snake (while in *Salât*) and he kills it, there is nothing on him unless his action takes a long time or he turns away from the *Qibla* (in the process) in which case he breaks his *Salât*.

Whoever is unsure whether he is in the *Witr* or the last *Rak'at* of *shaf'*, should make it the last *Rak'at* of *shaf'* and then do the *Sujud* after *Salaam* then the *Witr*. Whoever talks between

مختصر الأخضري

shaf' and *Al-Witr* forgetfully has nothing on him. If however, he does so deliberately it is abhorrent but there is still nothing on him.

One who joins *Salât* late and makes less than a *Rak'at* with the Imam does not do the *Sujud* of forgetfulness with him, be that before or after *Salaam*. If he therefore, does the *Sujud* with the Imam his *Salât* becomes invalid. If on the other hand, he makes a full *Rak'at* or more with the Imam, he does the *Sujud* before *Salaam* with him and delays the *Sujud* after *Salaam* until he completes his *Salât* and then makes it on his own. If he deliberately makes the after *Salaam Sujud* with the Imam, his *Salât* becomes invalid. If he does so forgetfully then he makes *Sujud* after *Salaam*.

If the one who joins *Salât* late forgets after the *Salaam* of his Imam he is like one making *Salât* alone. If such a person owes the after *Salaam Sujud* on account of his Imam and the before *Salaam Sujud* on his own account, the before *Salaam Sujud* would suffice him.

Whoever forgets the *Ruku'* and remembers while in *Sujud*, he should return standing and it is recommended that he repeats something of recitation and then goes to *Ruku'* and finally does the *Sujud* after *Salaam*.

Whoever forgets a *Sajda* and remembers after standing up, should return to the sitting position and go to *Sujud* except if he had already sat down before standing in which case he should not repeat the sitting. On the other hand, whoever, forgets two *Sujuds* should go back directly to *Sujud* without sitting and in all these situations he does the *Sujud* after *Salaam*.

مختصر الأخضري

If however, he remembers the *Sujud* after he has raised his head for the following *Rak'at*, he continues in his *Salât* and does not return. He then cancels the *Rak'at* in which the mistake occurred and adds another *Rak'at* in its place and then does the *Sujud* before *Salaam*. The same applies if at all this happened in the first two *Rak'at* and he remembered while already in the third *Rak'at* and after *Salaam*: also if it was not in the first two or if it was in them and he remembered before starting the third as the *Surah* and the sitting have not been missed.

Whoever pronounces the *Salaam* while unsure about the completion of his *Salât*, his *Salât* becomes invalid.

Forgetfulness in missed *Salats* being made up for, is the same as forgetfulness in *Salât* being observed on time.

FORGETFULNESS IN NAAFILAH

Forgetfulness in *Naafilah Salât* is like forgetfulness in *Fard Salât* except in six issues: *Al Fâtiha*, the *Surah*, silent and audible recitation, the addition of a *Rak'at* and forgetting some of the pillars: obligatory acts if it takes a long time.

Whoever forgets the *Fâtiha* in *Naafilah* and remembers after going to *Ruku'*, he continues and repairs this with the *Sujud* before *Salaam* as opposed to the *Fard Salât* where he will have to nullify that *Rak'at*, add another *Rak'at* and go ahead, then his *Sujud* would be as we mentioned in the case of one who omits the *Sujud*.

مختصر الأخضري

Whoever forgets the *Surah* or audible or silent recitation in *Naafilah* and remembers after

Ruku', he should continue and no *Sujuds* would be required of him as opposed to the *Fard*.

Whoever arises unto the third *Rak'at* in *Naafilah* and remembers before going to *Ruku'*, he should return sitting and do the *Sujud* after *Salaam*. If however, he has already gone to *Ruku'*, he continues and adds a fourth *Rak'at* and then does the *Sujud* before *Salaam*. This is as opposed to the *Fard* where he should return sitting at whichever point he remembers and then repairs it with the *Sujud* after *Salaam*.

Whoever forgets an obligatory element in *Naafilah* such as *Ruku'* or *Sujud* and does not remember until he has said the *Salaam* and a long time has passed, there would be no need for him to repeat it. This is again as opposed to *Fard Salât* in which case he would always have to repeat it.

Whoever intentionally cuts short his *Naafilah* or leaves out a *Rak'at* or a *Sajda* deliberately should always repeat it.

Whoever sighs in his *Salât* has nothing on him unless he distinctly articulates a letter.

FORGETFULNESS ON THE PART OF THE IMAM

If the Imam makes an error of omission or addition the follower(s) calls his attention by saying "*Subhâna'llâh*", Glory be to Allah.

مختصر الأخضري

When your Imam arises after two *Rak'at*, (without sitting first) say *Subhâna'llâh*! If however, he has already left the ground, follow him[40]. If he sits after the first or second *Rak'at*, arise and do not sit with him[41]. If he makes only one *Sajda* and leaves the second, say *Subhâna'llâh* and do not arise with him unless you fear he will go into *Ruku'* in which case you must follow him and do not after that sit with him neither in the second nor third *Rak'at*. When (he finally) makes *Salaam*, add another *Rak'at* in place of the *Rak'at* you cancelled thereby completing your *Salât* and do the *Sujud* before *Salaam*. If this happens in a congregation then it is best that you put one of you forward to complete the *Salât* with you.

If the Imam adds a third *Sajda*, say *Subhâna'llâh* and do not make the *Sujud* with him.

When the Imam arises unto a fifth *Rak'at*, he who is sure of its necessity should follow him; likewise he who is in doubt. He who is certain it is an addition should remain sitting. If the former sits and the latter arises then their *Salât* becomes invalid.

If the Imam pronounces the *Salaam* before the completion of the *Salât*, the one behind him should say *Subhâna'llâh*. If he (the Imam) believes him, he completes his *Salât* and does the *Sujud* after *Salaam*. If however, he has doubts about the information, he asks two trusted persons and it would be permissible for them to talk in this situation. If however, he is certain the *Salât* is complete he acts according to his certainty and leaves the two trusted ones unless there be many people behind him in which case he leaves his certainty and refers to them.

---

40 Remember in cases like this if he returns sitting then it is Sujud after Salaam. If he continues without sitting, it is Sujud before Salaam.

41 Here also you say Subhâna'llâh to call his attention to the error.

THE END

سلم الإمام قبل كمال الصلاة سبح به من خلفه ، فإن صدقه كمل صلاته وسجد بعد السلام ، وإن شك في خبره سأل عدلين وجاز لهما الكلام في ذلك ، وإن تيقن الكمال عمل على يقينه وترك العدلين إلا أن يكثر الناس خلفه فيترك يقينه ويرجع إليهم .

بحمد الله تعالى تم طبع كتاب [مختصر الأخضري]
مصححا بمعرفة لجنة العلماء برياسة : الشيخ أحمد سعد علي

وتذكر قبل عقد الثالثة لأن السورة والجلوس لم يفوتا. ومن سلم شاكاً في كمال صلاته بطلت صلاته ، والسهو في صلاة القضاء كالسهو في صلاة الأداء، والسهو في النافلة كالسهو في الفريضة إلا في ست مسائل : الفاتحة والسورة والسر والجهر ، وزيادة ركعة ونسيان بعض الأركان إن طال ، فمن نسي الفاتحة في النافلة وتذكر بعد الركوع تمادى وسجد قبل السلام بخلاف الفريضة ، فإنه يلغي تلك الركعة ويزيد أخرى ويتمادى ، ويكون سجوده كما ذكرنا في تارك السجود . ومن نسى السورة أو الجهر أو السر في النافلة وتذكر بعد الركوع تمادى ولا سجود عليه بخلاف الفريضة . ومن قام إلى ثالثة في النافلة فإن تذكر قبل عقد الركوع رجع وسجد بعد السلام ، وإن عقد الثالثة تمادى وزاد الرابعة وسجد قبل السلام بخلاف الفريضة فإنه يرجع متى ما ذكر ويجد بعد السلام ، ومن نسى ركناً من النافلة كالركوع أو السجود ولم يتذكر حتى سلم وطال فلا إعادة عليه بخلاف الفريضة فإنه يعيدها أبداً، ومن قطع النافلة عامداً أو ترك منا ركعة أو سجدة عامداً أعادها أبدا ، ومن تنهد في صلاته في شيء عليه إلا أن ينطق بحروف ، وإذا سها الإمام بنقص أو زيادة سبح به المأموم وإذا قام إمامك من ركعتين فسبح به ، فإن فارق الأرض فاتبعه ، وإن جلس في الأولى أو في الثالثة فقم ولا تجلس معه ، وإن سجد واحدة وترك الثانية فسبح به ولا تقم معه إلا أن تخاف عقد ركوعه فاتبعه ولا تجلس بعد ذلك معه لا في ثانية ولا في رابعة ،

أخرى أيضاً ، وحيث قضى الركعة فلا سجود عليه إلا أن يكون شاكاً في الركوع أو السجود ، ومن جاءته عقرب أو حية فقتلها فلا شيء عليه إلا أن يطول فعله أو يستدبر القبلة فإنه يقطع ومن شك هل هو في الوتر أو في ثانية الشفع جعلها ثانية الشفع وسجد بعد السلام ثم أوتر ، ومن تكلم بين الشفع والوتر ساهياً فلا شيء عليه ، وإن كان عامداً كره ولا شيء عليه ؛ والمسبوق إن أدرك مع الإمام أقل من ركعة فلا يسجد معه لا قبلياً ولا بعدياً فإن سجد معه بطلب صلاته ، وإن أدرك ركعة كاملة أو أكثر سجد معه القبلي وأخر البعدي حتى يتم صلاته فيسجد بعد سلامه ، فإن سجد مع الإمام عامداً بطلت صلاته وإن كان ساهياً سجد بعد السلام ، وإن سها المسبوق بعد سلام الإمام فهو كالمصلى وحده ، وإذا ترتب على المسبوق بعدي من جهة إمامه وقبلي من جهة نفسه أجزأه القبلي . ومن نسي الركوع وتذكره في السجود رجع قائماً، ويستحب له أن يعيد شيئاً من القراءة ثم يركع ويسجد بعد السلام ، ومن نسي سجدة واحدة وتذكرها بعد قيامه رجع جالساً وسجدها إلا أن يكون قد جلس قبل القيام فلا يعيد الجلوس، ومن نسي سجدتين خر ساجداً ولم يجلس ويسجد في جميع ذلك بعد السلام ، وإن تذكر السجود بعد رفع رأسه من الركعة التي تليها تمادى على صلاته ولم يرجع وألغى ركعة السهو وزاد ركعة في موضعها بانياً وسجد قبل السلام إن كان من الأوليين وتذكر بعد عقد الثالثة ، وبعد السلام إن لم تكن من الأوليين أو كانت منهما

بكلمة من غير القرآن سجد بعد السلام ، وإن كانت من القرآن فلا سجود عليه إلا يتغير اللفظ أو يفسد المعنى فيسجد بعد السلام، ومن نعس في الصلاة فلا سجود عليه ، وإن ثقل نومه أعاد الصلاة والوضوء ، وأنين المريض مغتفر والتنحنح للضرورة مغتفر ، وللإفهام منكر ولا تبطل الصلاة به ، ومن ناداه أحد فقال له : سبحانه الله كره وصحت صلاته ، ومن وقف في القراءة ولم يفتح عليه أحد ترك تلك الآية وقرأ ما بعدها ، فإن تعذرت عليه ركع . ولا ينظر مصحفاً بين يديه إلا أن يكون في الفاتحة فلابد من كمالها بمصحف أو غيره ، فإن ترك منها آية سجد قبل السلام ، وإن كان أكثر بطلت صلاته ، ومن فتح على غير إمامه بطلب صلاته ، ولا يفتح على إمامه إلا أن ينتظر الفتح أو يفسد المعنى ، ومن جال فكره قليلاً في أمور الدنيا نقص ثوابه ولم تبطل صلاته ، ومن دفع الماشي بين يديه أو سجد على شق جبهته أو سجد على طية أو طيتين من عمامته فلا شيء عليه ، ولا شيء في غلبة القيء والقلس في الصلاة ، وسهو المأموم يحمله الإمام إلا أن يكون من نقص الفريضة، وإذا سها المأموم أو نعس أو زوحم عن الركوع وهو في غير الأولى ، فإن طمع في إدراك الإمام قبل رفعه من السجدة الثانية ركع ولحقه ، وإن لم يطمع ترك الركوع وتبع إمامه وقضى ركعة في موضعها بعد سلام إمامه . وإن سها عن السجود أو زوحم أو نعس حتى قام الإمام إلى ركعة أخرى سجد أن طمع في إدراك الإمام قبل الركوع وإلا تركه وتبع الإمام وقضى ركعة

السلام ، وإن فات بالركوع سجد لترك الجهر قبل السلام ولترك السر بعد السلام سواه كان من الفاتحة أو السورة وحدها ، ومن ضحك في الصلاة بطلت سواء كان ساهياً أو عامداً ، ولا يضحك في صلاته إلا غافل متلاعب ، والمؤمن إذا قام لصلاة أعرض بقلبه عن كل ما سوى الله سبحانه وترك الدنيا وما فيها ، حتى يحضر بقلبه جلال الله سبحانه وعظمته ، ويرتعد قلبه وترهب نفسه من هيبة الله جل جلاله ، فهذه صلاة المتقين ولا شيء عليه في التبسم ، وبكاء الخاشع في الصلاة مغتفر ، ومن أنصت لمتحدث قليلاً فلا شيء عليه، ومن قام من ركعتين قبل الجلوس ، فإن تذكر قبل أن يفارق الأرض بيديه وركبتيه رجع إلى الجلوس ولا سجود عليه ، وإن فارقها تمادى ولم يرجع وسجد قبل السلام وإن رجع بعد المفارقة وبعد القيام ساهياً أو عامداً صحت صلاته وسجد بعد السلام ، ومن نفخ في صلاته ساهياً سجد بعد السلام ، وإن كان عامداً بطلت صلاته . ومن عطس في صلاته فلا يشتغل بالحمد ولا يرد على من شمته ولا يشمت عاطساً ، فإن حمد الله فلا شيء عليه . ومن تثاءب في الصلاة سد فاه ، ولا ينفث إلا في ثوبه من غير إخراج حروف ، ومن شك في حدث أو نجاسة فتفكر في صلاته قليلاً ، ثم تيقن الطهارة فلا شيء عليه ، ومن التفت في الصلاة ساهياً فلا شيء عليه ، وإن تعتمد فهو مكروه ، وإن استدبر القبلة قطع الصلاة ، ومن صلى بحرير أو ذهب أو سرق في الصلاة أو نظر محرما في عاص وصلاته صحيحة ، ومن غلط في القراءة

وأما السنة الواحدة فلا سجود لها إلا السر والجهر ، فمن أسر في الجهر سجد قبل السلام ، ومن جهر في السر سجد بعد السلام ، ومن تكلم ساهياً سجد بعد السلام ، ومن سلم من ركعتين ساهياً سجد بعد السلام ، ومن زاد في الصلاة ركعة أو ركعتين سجد بعد السلام ومن زاد في الصلاة مثلها بطلت ، ومن شك في كمال صلاته أتى بما شك فيه والشك في النقصان كتحققه ، فمن شك في ركعة أو سجدة أتى بها وسجد بعد السلام ، وإن شك في السلام سلم إن كان قريباً ولا سجود عليه ، وإن طال بطلت صلاته ، والموسوس يترك الوسوسة من قلبه ، ولا يأتي بما شك فيه ، ولكن يسجد بعد السلام سواء شك في زيادة أو نقصان ، ومن جهر في القنوت فلا سجود عليه ولكنه يكره عمده ، ومن زاد السورة في الركعتين الأخيرتين فلا سجود عليه ، ومن سمع ذكر محمد صلى الله عليه وآله وسلم وهو في الصلاة فصلى عليه فلا شيء عليه ، سواه كان ساهياً أو عامداً أو قائماً أو جالساً . ومن قرأ سورتين فأكثر في ركعة واحدة أو خرج من سورة إلى سورة ، أو ركع قبل تمام السورة فلا شيء عليه في جميع ذلك ، ومن أشار في صلاته بيده أو رأسه فلا شيء عليه ، ومن كرر الفاتحة ساهياً سجد بعد السلام ، وإن كان عامداً فالظاهر البطلان ، ومن تذكر السورة بعد انحنائه إلى الركوع فلا يرجع إليها ، ومن تذكر السر أو الجهر قبل الركوع أعاد القراءة ، فإن كان ذلك في السورة وحدها أعادها ولا سجود عليه ، وإن كان في الفاتحة أعادها وسجد بعد

بمفرط ويقضيها على نحو ما فاتته إن كان حضرية قضاها حضرية ، وإن كان سفرية قضاها سفرية سواء كان حين القضاء في حضر أو سفر ، والترتيب بين الحاضرتين وبين يسير الفوائت مع الحاضرة واجب مع الذكر ، واليسير أربع صلوات فأدنى ، ومن كانت عليه أربع صلوات فأقل صلاها قبل الحاضرة ولو خرج وقتها ، ويجوز القضاء في كل وقت ؛ ولا يتنقل من عليه القضاء ولا يصلي الضحى ولا قيام رمضان ولا يجوز له إلا الشفع والوتر والفجر والعيدان والخسوف والاستسقاء ويجوز لمن عليهم القضاء أن يصلوا جماعة إذا استوت صلاتهم ومن نسي عدد ما عليه من القضاء صلى عدداً لا يبقى معه شك .

باب في السهو

وسجود السهو في الصلاة سنة فللنقصان سجدتان قبل السلام بعد تمام التشهدين يزيد بعدهما تشهداً آخر ، وللزيادة سجدتان بعد السلام يتشهد بعدها ويسمل تسليمة أخرى ، ومن نقص وزاد سجد قبل السلام ، ومن نسي السجود القبلي حتى سلم سجد إن كان قريباً ، وإن طال أو خرج من المسجد بطل السجود . وتبطل الصلاة معه إن كان على ثلاث سنن أو أكثر من ذلك وإلا فلا تبطل ، ومن نسي السجود البعدي سجده ولو بعد عام ، ومن نقص فريضة فلا يجزيه السجود عنها ، ومن نقص الفضائل

الصلاة خشوع وتواضع لله سبحانه بالقيام والركوع والسجود وإجلال وتعظيم له بالتكبير والتسبيح والذكر فحافظ على صلاتك فإنها أعظم العبادات ، ولا تترك الشيطان يلعب بقلبك ويشغلك عن صلاتك حتى يطمس قلبك ويحرمك من لذة أنوار الصلاة ، فعليك بدوام الخشوع فيها فإنها تنهى عن الفحشاء والمنكر بسبب الخشوع فيها ، فاستعن بالله أنه خير مستعان .

(فصل) للصلاة المفروضة سبعة أحوال مرتبة تؤدي عليها : أربعة منها على الوجوب ، وثلاثة على الاستحباب : أولها القيام بغير استناد ثم القيام باستناد ، ثم الجلوس بغير استناد ، ثم الجلوس باستناد . فالترتيب بين هذه الأربعة على الوجوب إذا قدر على حالة منها وصلى بحالة دونها ، بطلت صلاته ، والثلاثة التي على الاستحباب هي : أن يصلي العاجز عن هذه الثلاثة المذكورة على جنبه الأيمن ، ثم على الأيسر ثم على ظهره ؛ فإن خالف في الثلاثة لم يبطل صلاته والاستناد الذي تبطل به صلاة القادر على تركه هو الذي يسقط بسقوطه ، وإن كان لا يسقط بسقوطه فهو مكروه ، وأما النافلة فيجوز للقادر على القيام أن يصليها جالساً ، وله نصف أجر القائم ويجوز أن يدخلها جالساً ويقوم بعد ذلك أو يدخلها قائماً ويجلس بعد ذلك إلا أن يدخلها بنية القيام فيها فيمتنع جلوسه بعد ذلك .

(فصل) يجب قضاء ما في الذمة من الصلوات ولا يحل التفريط فيها ، ومن صلى كل يوم خمسة أيام فليس فليس

تعالى عليه وكل اله وسلم ، والسجود على الانف والكفين والركبتين وأطراف القدمين والسترة لغير المأموم وأقلها غلظ رمح وطول ذراع طاهر ثابت غير مشوش.

(وفضائلها) رفع اليدين عند الإحرام حتى تقابلا الأذنين وقول المأموم والفذ : ربنا ولك الحمد ، والتأمين بعد الفاتحة للفذ والمأموم ، ولا يقولها الإمام إلا في قراءة السر ، والتسبيح في الركوع والدعاء في السجود ، وتطويل القراءة في الصبح والظهر تليها وتقصيرها في العصر والمغرب، وتوسطها في العشاء وتكون السورة الأولى قبل الثانية وأطول منها ، والهيئة المعلومة في الركوع والسجود والجلوس ، والقنوت سراً قبل الركوع وبعد السورة في ثانية الصبح، ويجوز الركوع، والدعاء بعد التشهد الثاني ، ويكون التشهد الثاني أطول من الأول والتيامن بالسلام وتحريك السبابة في التشهد ، ويكره الالتفات في الصلاة ، وتغميض العينين ، والبسملة والتعوذ في الفريضة ، ويجوزان في النقل ، والوقوف على رجل واحدة إلا أن يطول قيامه ، واقتران رجليه وجعل درهم أو غيره في فمه ، وكذلك كل ما يشوشه في جيبه أو كمه و على ظهره ، والتفكر في أمور الدنيا وكل ما يشغله عن الخشوع في الصلاة .

(فصل) للصلاة نور عظيم تشرق به قلوب المصلين ولا يناله إلا الخاشعون ، فإذا أتيت إلى الصلاة ففرغ قلبك من الدنيا وما فيها ، واشتعل بمراقبة موالاك الذي تصلى لوجهه واعتقد أن

وشرط الصلاة طهارة الحديث وطهارة الخبث من البدن والثوب والمكان وستر العورة واستقبال القبلة ، وترك الكلام وترك الأفعال الكثيرة ، وعورة الرجل ما بين السرة إلى الركبة والمرأة كلها عورة ما عدا الوجه والكفين ، وتكره الصلاة في السراويل لا إذا كان فوقها شيء ، ومن تنجس ثوبه ولم يجد ثوباً غيره ولم يجد ماء يغسله به أو لم يكن عنده ما يلبس حتى يغسله خروج الوقت صلى فيه بنجاسته ، ولا يحل تأخير الصلاة لعدم الطهارة ؛ ومن فعل ذلك فقد عصى ربه ، ومن لم يجد ما يستر به عورته صلى عرياناً ؛ ومن أخطأ القبلة أعاد في الوقت ، وكل إعادة في الوقت فهي فضيلة ، وكل ما تعاد منه الصلاة في الوقت فلا تعاد منه الفائتة والنافلة .

(فصل) فرائض الصلاة : نية الصلاة المعينة ، وتكبيرة الإحرام والقيام لها ، والفاتحة والقيام لها ، والركوع ، والرفع منه والسجود على الجبهة ، والرفع منه ، والاعتدال ، والطمأنينة، والترتيب بين فرائضها ، والسلام ، وجلوسه الذي يقارنه .

(وشرط النية) : مقارنتها لتكبيرة الإحرام .

(وسنتها) الإقامة ، والسورة التي بعد الفاتحة ، والقيام لها ، والسر فيما يسر فيه ، والجهر فيما يجهر فيه ، وسمع الله لمن حمده وكل تكبيرة سنة إلا الأولى ، والتشهدان والجلوس لهما ، وتقديم الفاتحة على السورة والتسليمة الثانية والثالثة للمأموم والجهر بالتسليمة الواجبة ، والصلاة على رسول الله صلى الله

فصل في النفاس

والنفاس كالحيض في منعه ، وأكثره ستون يوماً ، فإذا انقطع الدم قبلها ولو في يوم الولادة اغتسلت وصلت . فإذا عاودها الدم فإن كان بينهما خمسة عشر يوماً فأكثر كان الثاني حيضا ، وإلا ضم إلى الأول وكان من تمام النفاس .

فصل في الأوقات

الوقت المختار للظهر من زوال الشمس إلى آخره القامة ، والمختار للعصر من القامة إلى الأصفرار وضروريهما إلى الغروب والمختار لمغرب قد ما تصلى فيه بعد شروطها ، والمختار للعشاء من مغيب الشفق إلى ثلث الليل الأول ، وضروريهما إلى طلوع الفجر ؛ والمختار للصبح من الفجر إلى الإسفار الأعلى وضرورية إلى طلوع الشمس ، والقضاء في الجميع ما وراء ذلك ، ومن آخر الصلاة حتى خرج وقتها فعليه ذنب عظيم إلا أن يكون ناسياً أو نائماً ؛ ولا تصلى نافلة بعد صلاة الصبح إلى ارتفاع الشمس ، وبعد صلاة العصر إلى صلاة المغرب ، وبعد طلوع الفجر إلا الورد لنائم عنه وعند جلوس إمام الجمعة على المنبر وبعد والجمعة حتى يخرج من المسجد.

فصل في شروط الصلاة

والحصير والخشب والحشيش ونحوه ، ورخص للمريض في حائط الحجر والطوب إن لم يجد مناولاً غيره .

(وسننه) : تجديد الصعيد ليديه ومسح ما بين الكوعين والمرفقين ، والترتيب .

(وفضائله) التسمية وتقديم اليمنى على اليسرى وتقديم ظاهر الذراع على باطنه ومقدمة على مؤخره .

(ونواقضه) : كالوضوء ولا تصلى فريضتان بتيمم واحد ، ومن تيمم لفرضة جاز له النوافق بعدها ومس المصحف والطواف والتلاوة إن نوى ذلك واتصلت بالصلاة ولم يخرج الوقت؛ وجاز بتيمم النافلة كل ما ذكر إلا الفريضة ، ومن صلى العشاء بتيمم قام للشفع والوتر بعدها من غير تأخير ، ومن تيمم من جنابة فلابد من نيتها .

فصل في الحيض

والنساء مبتدأة ومعتادة وحامل ، وأكثر الحيض للمبتدأة خمسة عشر يوماً وللمعتادة عادتها، فإن تمادى بها الدم زادت ثلاثة أيام ما لم تجاوز خمسة عشر يوماً ، وللحامل بعد ثلاثة أشهر خمسة عشر يوماً ونحوها ، وبعد ستة أشهر عشرون ونحوها ، فإن تقطع الدم لفقت أيامه حتى تكمل عادتها ، ولا يحل للحائض صلاة ولا صوم ولا طواف ولا مس مصحف ولا دخول مسجد، وعليها

(وسننه) : غسل اليدين إلى الكوعين كالوضوء ، والمضمضة والاستنشاق والاستنثار، وغسل صماخ الأذن ، وهي الثقبة الداخلة في الرأس ، وأما صحفة الأذن فيجب غسل ظاهرها وباطنها .

(وفضائله) : البداية بغسل النجاسة ثم الذكر فينوي عنده ثم أعضاء الوضوء مرة مرة ، ثم أعلى جسده ، وتثليث غسل الرأس ، وتقديم شق جسده الأيمن ، وتقليل الماء على الأعضاء ، ومن نسي لمعة أو عضوا من غسله بادر إلى غسل حين تذكره ولو بعد شهر ، وأعاد ما صلى قبله. وإن آخره بعد ذكره بطل غسله ، فإن كان في أعضاء الوضوء وصادفه غسل الوضوء أجزأه .

(فصل) لا يحل للجنب دخول المسجد ، ولا قراءة القرآن إلا الآية ونحوها للتعوذ ونحوه ، ولا يجوز لمن لا يقدر على الماء البارد أن يأتي زوجته حتى يعد الآلة إلا أن يحتلم ، فلا شيء عليه .

فصل في التيمم

ويتيمم المسافر في غير معصية ، والمريض لفريضة أو نافلة ، ويتيمم الحاضر الصحيح للفرائض إذا خاف خروج وقتها ، ولا يتيمم الحاضر الصحيح لنافلة ولا جمعة ولا جنازة إلا إذا تعينت عليه الجنازة .

(وفرائض التيمم) : النية والصعيد الطاهر ، ومسح الوجه ومسح اليدين إلى الكوعين ، وضربة الأرض الأولى والفور ، ودخول الوقت واتصاله بالصلاة ؛ والصعيد : هو التراب والطوب والحجر ، والثلج والخضخاض ونحو ذلك . ولا يجوز بالجص المطبوخ

(فصل) نواقض الوضوء أحدث وأسباب : فالأحداث : البول والغائط والريح والمذى والودى . والأسباب : النوم الثقيل والإغماء والسكر والجنون والقبلة ، ولمس المرأة إن قصد اللذة أو وجدها ، ومس الذكر بباطن الكف أو بباطن الأصابع ؛ ومن شك في حدث وجب عليه الوضوء إلا أن يكون موسوساً فلا شيء عليه ، ويجب عليه غسل الذكر كله من المذى ، ولا يغسل الانثيين والمذى : هو الماء الخارج عند الشهوة الصغرى بتفكر أو نظر أو غيره .

(فصل) لا يحل لغير المتوضي صلاة ولا طواف ولا مس نسخة القرآن العظيم ولا جلدها، لا بيده ولا بعود ونحوه إلا الجزء منها المتعلم فه ، ولا مس لوح القرآن العظيم على غير الوضوء إلا لمتعلم فيه أو معلم يصححه ؛ والصبى في مس القرآن كالكبير والإثم على مناوله له ، ومن صلى بغير وضوء عامداً فهو كافر والعياذ بالله .

(فصل) يجب الغسل من ثلاثة أشياء : الجنابة والحيض والنفاس ، فالجنابة قسمان : أحدهما خروج المني بلذة معتادة في نوم أو يقظة بجماع أو غيره . والثاني : مغيب الحشفة في الفرج، ومن رأى في منامه كأنه يجامع ولم يخرج منه مني فلا شيء عليه ، ومن وجد في ثوبه منياً يابساً لا يدري متى أصابه ، اغتسل وأعاد ما صلى من آخر نومه نامها فيه .

(فصل) فرائض الغسل : النية عند الشروع والفور والدلك والعموم .

(فصل) إذا تعينت النجاسة غسل محلها ، فإن التبست غسل الثوب كله ، ومن شك في إصابة النجاسة نضح ، وإن إصابة شيء شك في نجاسته فلا نضح عليه ، ومن تذكر النجاسة وهو في الصلاة قطع إلا أن يخاف خروج الوقت ، ومن صلى بها ناسياً وتذكر بعد السلام أعد في الوقت .

(فصل) فرائض الوضوء سبع : النية ، وغسل الوجه ، وغسل اليدين إلى المرفقين ، ومسح الرأس ، وغسل الرجلين إلى الكعبين ، والدلك ، والفور .

(وسننه) غسل اليدين إلى الكوعين عند الشروع ، والمضمضة ، والاستنشاق ، والاستنثار، ورد مسح الرأس ومسح الأذنين وتجديد الماء لهما ، والترتيب بين الفرئض ؛ ومن نسى فرضاً من أعضائه ، فإن تذكره بالقرب فعله وما بعده ، وإن طال فعله وحده وأعاد ما صلى قبله ، وإن ترك سنة فعلها ولا يعيد الصلاة ، ومن نسى لمعة غسلها وحدها بنية ، وإن صلى قبل ذلك أعاد ، ومن تذكر المضمضة والاستنشاق بعد أن شرع في الوجه فلا يرجع إليهما حتى يتم وضوءه .

(وفضائله) التسمية والسواك والزائد على الغسلة الأولى في الوجه واليدين ، والداءه بمقدم الرأس، وترتيب السنن وقله الماء على العضو ، وتقديم اليمنى على السيرى ، ويجب تخليل أصابع الرجلين ، ويجب تخليل اللحية الخفيفة في الوضوء دون الكثيفة ، ويجب تخليلها في الغسل ولو كانت كثيفة .

المنكر ، ويحرم عليه الكذب والغيبة والنميمة والكبر والعجب والرياء والسمعة والحسد والبغض والسخرية والزنا والنظر إلى الأجنبية والتلذذ بكلامها وأكل أموال الناس بغير طيب نفس والأكل الشفاعة أو الدين وتأخير الصلاة عن أوقاتها . ولا يحل له صحبة فاسق ولا مجالسته لغير ضرورة ، ولا يطلب رضا المخلوقين بسخط الخالد ، قال الله سبحانه وتعالى : (والله ورسوله أحق أن يرضوه إن كانوا مؤمنين) وقال عليه الصلاة والسلام : "لا طاعة لمخلوق في معصية الخالق" ولا يحل له أن يفعل فعلاً حتى يعلم حكم الله فيه ويسأل العلماء ويقتدي بالمتبعين لسنة صلى الله عليه وسلم الذين يدلون على طاعة الله ، ويحذرون من اتباع الشيطان ولا يرضى لنفسه ما رضيه المفلسون الذين ضاعت أعمارهم في غير طاعة الله تعالى، فيا حسرتهم ويا يطول بكائهم يوم القيامة نسأل الله أن يوفقنا لاتباع سنة نبينا وشفيعنا وسيدنا محمد صلى الله عليه وسلم .

فصل في الطهارة

الطهارة قسمان : طهارة حدث وطهارة خبث ، ولا يصح الجميع إلا بالماء الطاهر المطر ، وهو الذي لم يتغير لونه أو طعمه أو رائحته بما يفارقه غالباً كالزيت والسمن والدسم كله ، والوذح والصابون والوسخ ونحوه ، ولا بأس التراب والحماة والسبخة والأجر ونحوه .

" تلك حدود الله فلا تعدوها "
(قرآن كريم)

بسم الله الرحمن الرحيم

الحمد لله رب العالمين ، والصلاة والسلام على سيدنا محمد خاتم النبيين وإمام المرسلين وعلى آله وصحبه أجمعين .

(أول ما يجب على المكلف) : تصحيح إيمانه ثم معرفة ما يصلح به فرض عينه كأحكام الصلاة والطهارة والصيام . (ويجب) عليه أن يحافظ على حدود الله ويقف عند أمره ونهيه ويتوب إلى الله سبحانه قبل أن يسخط عليه . (وشروط التوبة) الندم على ما فات ، والنية أن لا يعود إلى ذنب فيما بقى عليه من عمره ، وأن يترك المعصية في ساعتها إن كان متلبسا بها ، ولا يحل له أن يؤخر التوبة ، ولا يقول حتى يهديني الله ؛ فإنه من علامات الشقاء والخذلان وطمس البصيرة.

(ويجبُ) عليه حفظ لسانه من الفحشاء والمنكر والكلام القبيح وإيمان الطلاق ، وانتهار المسلم وإهانته ، وسبه وتخويفه في غير حق شرعي .

(ويجبُ) عليه حفظ بصره عن ا لنظر إلى الحرام ، ولا يحل له أن ينظر إلى مسلم بنظرة تؤذيه إلا أن يكون فاسقاً فيجب هجرانه .

(ويجب) عليه حفظ جميع جوارحه ما استطاع ، وأن يحب لله ويبغض له ويرضى له ويغضب له ، وبأمر بالمعروف وينهى عن

مختصر الأخضري

مختصر الاخضري

في

العبـــادات

على

مذهب الإمام مالك

تأليف

أبي زيد عبد الرحمن بن محمد الصغير الاخضري

(من علماء القرن العاشر الهجري)

الطبعة الثالثة

1374هـ - 1955م

نشر ملتقى أهل الحديث

شركة مكتبة ومطبعة مصطفى الحلبي وأولاده بمصر

www.ingramcontent.com/pod-product-compliance
Lightning Source LLC
Chambersburg PA
CBHW070551300426
44113CB00011B/1866